Ladies' Aid Society

Our Cook Book

Ladies' Aid Society

Our Cook Book

ISBN/EAN: 9783744792509

Printed in Europe, USA, Canada, Australia, Japan

Cover: Foto ©Andreas Hilbeck / pixelio.de

More available books at **www.hansebooks.com**

OUR COOK BOOK.

PUBLISHED BY THE

LADIES' AID SOCIETY

OF THE FIFTH STREET BAPTIST CHURCH,

LOWELL, MASS.

"We may live without poetry, music and art;
We may live without conscience, and live without heart;
We may live without friends; we may live without books;
But civilized man cannot live without cooks.
He may live without books,—what is knowledge but grieving?
He may live without hope,—what is hope but deceiving?
He may live without love,—what is passion but pining?
But where is the man that can live without dining?"

—[OWEN MEREDITH.

FROM THE PRESS OF
ADAMS & FARLEY, 83 MIDDLE STREET, LOWELL, MASS.
1888.

Dear Friends :

This book is gotten out by the LADIES AID SOCIETY of the Fifth Street Baptist Church of Lowell. Our object has been the old one—to make some money. We have recarpeted our Church, and by this means have tried to help pay for it. We are gratified at our success. Our task has been arduous, for it has involved hard work, but it has been a pleasant one. We have made many acquaintances and have been treated with almost uniform courtesy. We thank our advertisers for their generous response to our call. We sincerely hope their investment will be profitable. We are sure it will, if they let their wives have a copy of this book. for men, we are told, do like a good dinner. For ourselves, we know better than ever whom to patronize, and to whom to refer our husbands and friends. We also thank the friends who buy the book. May it enlarge their culinery vision! And so we launch our little book upon the sea, hoping its esculent suggestions may find safe harbor in many a larder, and gather smiles and benedictions around many a well filled board.

LADIES' AID SOCIETY.

BREAD, ETC.

Corn Bread.

Two cups Indian meal, two cups flour, one tablespoon butter, two tablespoons sugar, one pint sweet milk, one egg, a little salt, one teaspoon soda, two of cream of tartar. Bake twenty minutes in small cake pans. If sour or butter milk is used, one teaspoon soda but no cream of tartar.

H. Merriam.

Pop Overs.

One cup milk, two cups flour, one egg, one teaspoon soda, two of cream tartar, three tablespoons sugar, two table spoons melted butter. Oven not over hot.

H. Merriam.

Graham Muffins.

One cup graham flour, one cup wheat flour, one and a half cups milk, two tablespoons sugar, two teaspoons baking powder and a little salt. Have your pans hot and bake in a quick oven.

Mrs. B. B. Hart.

Indian Cake.

One cup each of Indian meal and flour, one-half cup sugar, one fourth cup cream, two teaspoons baking powder, one teaspoon salt. Mix a little stiffer than for fritters.

Mrs. F. W. Cobb.

Potato Yeast.

Four large boiled potatoes mashed fine, one pint boiling water, two tablespoons brown sugar, one of salt. When partly cool add yeast.

K.

Rye Drop Cakes.

One pint sour milk, three eggs, one scant teaspoon soda, a little salt and rye meal, to make a batter that will spread a little but will not run. Drop with a spoon into round tins and bake fifteen minutes.

Mrs. M. C. Cole.

R. I. Brown Bread.

Three cups Indian meal, two cups flour, one cup molasses, one quart milk, one teaspoon soda. Pour into a two quart dish and steam from three to five hours

MRS. A. G. KIRBY.

Parker House Rolls.

One half cup yeast, and half cake dry yeast, two quarts flour, one pint boiled milk (cooled), two tablespoons sugar, two of lard and a little salt. Make a batter of part of flour and let rise, then stir in the rest of the flour and rise again. Make into rolls, placing a small piece of butter between the folds and rise again.

Q.

Flour Gems.

Two cups of flour, one cup milk, one cup water, one half teaspoon of soda, one teaspoon cream tartar, a little salt, mix well, and pour into hot gem pans.

MRS. J. BARNARD BROWN.

Brown Bread.

Two cups sour milk, two-thirds cup molasses, one teaspoon salt, one large teaspoon soda, flour, rye and corn meal each one half cup. Place in pail and boil five hours.

X.

LUMBER,

PICKLES, ETC.

Cucumber Pickles.

One bushel of fresh cucumbers, one cup salt. Place in a vessel a layer of cucumbers and sprinkle salt over them. Repeat the process until all are used. Pour on boiling water to cover them. Cover closely and let stand until morning. Then drain off the water and cover with boiling vinegar spiced to taste. Cover closely till cold, when they are ready for use. Two or three green peppers improve them.

MRS. M. I. SHATTUCK.

Chili Sauce.

Take eighteen large ripe tomatoes, three green peppers, and a large onion chopped fine, one and a half cups vinegar, one half cup sugar, one tablespoon salt, one teaspoon ginger and cinnamon. Boil one hour.

MRS. M. I. SHATTUCK.

Chili Sauce, No. 2.

Three pounds tomatoes, one onion chopped fine, two green peppers chopped fine seeds and all, two cups vinegar, two tablespoons sugar, one tablespoon each of salt, ginger, mustard, ground cloves, and half a tablespoon nutmeg. Boil three quarters of an hour.

A FRIEND.

Spiced Currants.

Five pounds currants, four pounds sugar, one pint vinegar, two table spoons each of cloves and allspice. Boil three hours.

A FRIEND.

Ketchup.

Eighteen ripe tomatoes, one onion, one cup sugar, two and a half cups vinegar, two teaspoons salt, one teaspoon each of cinnamon, ginger and cayenne pepper. Cook the tomatoes and onion until well done, strain, add vinegar &c, and cook thirty minutes.

MRS. F. W. COBB.

Chow-Chow.

One peck of green tomatoes chopped fine: add one half tea-cup of salt and let it stand over night. In the morning drain off the water, add one onion and two green peppers chopped fine, also dessert spoonful of cinnamon, clove, allspice, mustard and ginger and one half cup sugar. Cover with vinegar and cook one hour.

MRS. F. W. COBB.

Old Virginia, Chow-Chow.

Three pecks of ripe tomatoes, three of green tomatoes, five large heads of cabbage, one dozen large onions, one dozen ripe peppers, half a pound of celery. Chop very fine, cover with salt and soak twenty-four hours, then drain off brine, thoroughly cover with strong vinegar and add three pounds of sugar. Scald one hour, add one cup grated horse radish, two tablespoons white mustard seed, one of cloves, two of allspice, one of ginger, and one of ground mustard. Cover closely and set away for a month. This is excellent.

MISS C. LONG.

Chili Sauce, No. 3.

Peel and chop twelve large ripe tomatoes, two onions, add two tablespoons salt, two of sugar and four cups vinegar. Boil from two to four hours.

K.

Onion Pickle.

One peck of onions soaked in salt and water over night. In the morning peel them, put in milk and water, set on the stove to simmer, then put in bottles, add vinegar and stop tightly.

MRS. COBURN.

Pickled Mackerel.

Three dozen small mackerel, clean aud wipe dry. Mix together the following: One cup salt, one tablespoon allspice, one tablespoon cloves. Open each fish and sprinkle with above mixture, place in layers in stone jar sprinkling each layer with mixture. Heat enough cider vinegar to cover; pour on while hot, cover closely and bake five hours. Let this stand 24 hours before serving. Eat with lemon juice like sardines.

*

PIES.

Lemon Pies.

One cup boiling water, one tablespoon corn starch dissolved in cold water and stirred into the boiling. Remove from stove and add one cup sugar, and butter the size of an egg. When cold add one egg well beaten, the juice of one lemon and a part of the grated rind. This makes a large pie.

DELLA A. BEAN.

Lemon Pie No. 2.

Beat well together one egg, one cup sugar, pinch of salt, and the juice of one lemon, dissolve one tablespoon corn starch in a little cold water and pour over it one cup boiling water. Add one teaspoon butter and the grated peel of the lemon. Stir well together and bake with two crusts, wetting the top crust with milk.

F. M. C.

Lemon Pie, No. 3

One cup sugar, one lemon, the yolks of two eggs, a tablespoon of flour, a cup of milk. Frost with the whites.

MISS. C. LONG.

Lemon Pie, No 4

Grate four large apples with the pulp and juice of two lemons, add two eggs and one cup of sugar. This makes two pies.

MRS. S. M. MILLIKEN.

Cream Pie.

Three eggs, one cup sugar, three tablepoons cold water, one teaspoon cream of tartar, one half teaspoon soda, one and one half cups flour, and a little salt.

Cream. Two eggs, three tablespoons sugar, two tablespoons of corn starch. Beat well together and pour in one pint boiling milk. This makes two pies.

MRS. C. W. NEVERS.

Cream or Cocoanut Pies.

Two eggs, one cup sugar, one half cup water, one half teaspoon soda dissolved in the water, one teaspoon of cream of tartar, one and a half cups flour, and a small lump of butter.

Cream. One half cup sugar, one half cup flour, one egg. Beat the egg, stir in sugar and flour, stir in a half pint boiling milk, and two tablespoons cocoanut. Frost it and sprinkle thickly with cocoanut before dry.

ROSCOE B. THOMAS.

Lemon Custard Pie.

Three eggs, three tablespoons of boiled milk, one cup sugar, the juice of one lemon. Leave the whites of two eggs for frosting. Mix the ingredients, adding the milk last. Bake as custard. When done beat the whites of the eggs with a fork, spread over the top, and return to the oven to brown.

MRS. F. W. COBB.

Washington Pie.

One tablespoon butter, one cup sugar, one egg, one cup milk, one teaspoon lemon, two teaspoons cream of tartar. one teaspoon soda sifted with two and a half cups flour. Fill with jelly or cream, frost the top, and sprinkle on freshly grated cocoanut.

F. M. C.

Sponge Cream Pie.

Three eggs, one cup sugar, one and a half cups flour, two teaspoons Royal baking powder, one half cup cold water. Just before putting in oven add one tablespoon hot water.

Cream. One egg, one quarter pint milk, one quarter cup sugar, one quarter cup flour. Salt and flavor after cooking.

MRS. LUCY E. SHAW.

Beef Pie.

Take cold roast beef or steak, cut into thin slices, and put a layer into a deep pie dish with flour, pepper and salt and chopped onion or tomato. Place beef and seasoning in alternate layers until the dish is full. If you have gravy put it in, if not put in butter and water to make gravy. Mash one dozen boiled potatoes with half a cup of cream or milk, a little butter and salt. Spread over the pie, brush over with egg, and bake twenty minutes.

MRS. M. C. COLE.

COOKIES.

Cookies.

Two cups sugar, one cup butter, two eggs, one half cup milk, one teaspoon cream of tartar, one half teaspoon soda and flour to roll stiff.

F. M. C.

Ginger Snaps.

One pint molasses, one cup shortening, one tablespoon ginger. Put in tin dish and let boil thin. Set away to cool. When nearly cold add two teaspoons soda and a little salt, stir until it foams and use flour enough to roll.

MRS. COBURN.

Jumbles.

Two eggs, one cup sugar, one cup butter, one half cup sweet milk, one teaspoon soda and flour to roll.

K.

Cookies.

Two eggs, one cup sugar, one half cup butter, three tablespoons milk, one teaspoon cream of tartar, one half teaspoon soda. Roll very soft and flavor to taste.

K.

Sugar Cookies.

Two cups sugar, one cup butter, one half cup sour milk, one half teaspoon soda, flour to mix stiff. Roll thin and bake quickly.

MRS. SYLVESTER BEAN.

Ginger Snaps.

Bring to a scald one cup of molasses and stir in one tablespoon of soda. Pour it while foaming over one cup of sugar, one egg and one tablespoon ginger beaten together, then add one tablespoon vinegar, and flour enough to roll stirred in as lightly as possible.

H.

Cookies.

Two cups sugar, one cup butter, four eggs, one half cup milk, two teaspoons cream of tartar, one of soda, and one of ginger. Flour to roll. Bake quickly.

MRS. PALMER.

Ginger Snaps.

One cup sugar, one egg, two cups molasses, one half cup shortening, salt, table spoon ginger, one half cup cold water, small tablespoon soda. Make stiff with flour, roll quickly and bake slowly. This will make a large six quart pan full.

K.

Molasses Cookies.

One cup boiled molasses, one cup sugar, one tablespoon vinegar, two tablespoons water, one egg, one heaping teaspoon soda, and a little salt. Beat the sugar and egg together, then turn in the boiling molasses. Add the vinegar and water with the soda in it. Flour enough to roll.

MRS. LUCY E. SHAW.

Creams and Custards.

Floating Island.

Put one and a half pints of milk into a dish of hot water to heat. When boiling hot lay on the top of it the beaten whites of two eggs, let them cook fifteen minutes, turning over once. Then skim out into a pudding dish, and make a boiled custard of the milk, the yolks of the eggs with one whole one added, and one half cup of sugar. Flavor and turn over the whites.

MRS. WELLS.

Whipped Cream.

Put one pint nice cream into a bowl, whip with egg beater until stiff enough to cut with a knife, add one half cup sugar, one teaspoon vanilla. Whip all together, turn into a mould, and set away in a cool place until next day. It may be put in an ice chest and used the same day, but it is better if kept overnight.

MRS. C.

Apple Float.

Take one pint stewed apple, whites of three eggs beaten to a stiff froth, four tablespoons sugar, beat all together till stiff enough to stand alone. Fill a deep dish with boiled custard, pile the float on top and serve.

DELLA A. BEAN.

Apple Foam.

Pare, core and boil till soft six juicy apples, beat the whites of two eggs to a stiff froth, add three tablespoons powdered sugar. Beat thoroughly, the more the better. Flavor to taste.

MRS. S. M. SHATTUCK.

Apple Custard.

Pare, core, cook, and strain through a sieve eight juicy apples, add a half cup sugar and the grated rind and juice of one lemon. Put in a deep dish, and when cold turn over it a custard made of the yolks of four eggs, one half cup sugar and a pint of milk. Frost with the whites of the eggs and four tablespoons sugar.

F. M. C.

Tapioca Cream.

Cover three tablespoons of tapioca with water, and let it stand over night. In the morning pour off the water, and put the tapioca into one quart of milk over the fire. When it boils stir in the yolks of three eggs, two thirds of a cup of sugar and a little salt. Stir until it begins to thicken. Make a frosting of the whites of the eggs and spread on top, sprinkle with sugar and brown in the oven.

MRS. S. M. MILLIKEN.

Rice Cream.

One quart milk, three eggs, one half cup rice, one lemon, one teaspoon salt, one half cup sugar; steam the rice, milk, and salt together until rice is soft; beat the yolks of eggs with one tablespoon sugar and the grated rind of the lemon. When the rice is soft, take from steamer and add yolks, stirring until it thickens. Pour into dish. Beat whites with rest of sugar and lemon, put on top and brown in oven.

F. M. C.

GINGER BREAD.

Soft Ginger Bread, No. 1.

Dissolve one teaspoon of soda in one cup of boiling water, pour this mixture upon a piece of lard the size of an egg, add one cup molasses, one teaspoon ginger and a little salt. Mix soft and bake quickly.

MRS. J. B. BROWN.

Soft Gingerbread, No. 2.

Six cups flour, two cups molasses or sugar, one and a half cups milk, two teaspoons each of ginger and soda, a half cup lard. Bake slowly.

MRS. J. B. BROWN.

Hard Gingerbread.

One cup each of sugar and molasses, one half cup each of milk, cream, and butter, one teaspoon each of ginger, cream of tartar and soda, two eggs, and flour to mould.

MRS. PALMER.

Molasses Gingerbread.

One half cup sugar, one half cup molasses and of sour cream, one teaspoon each of soda and ginger, two cups flour, a pinch of salt. When all is well mixed, add one well beaten egg.

MRS. PALMER.

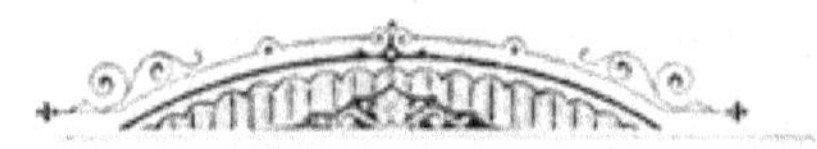

SOUPS.

Good Soup.

Take a marrow bone weighing four pounds meat and all, put in a kettle with cold water enough to cover it; when it begins to boil, skim thoroughly, add a very little salt to bring up the scum. When it has cooked about three hours, add more salt and pepper. About two hours before the soup is done, take three large sized yellow turnips, slice them thin, cut in squares and put in kettle, also six medium sized onions sliced up, also three sliced carrots, and three quarts of sliced potatoes. Take two slices of home made bread, cut up in thin squares, and add to the mixture when nearly done. Have sufficient stock by adding water to make as thin as desirable. Pepper and salt to taste. Cook until done. This will feed six persons, provided that they have good appetites.

Mrs. A. R. Abbott.

Cakes for Soup.

Break one egg into flour and mix to roll. Roll very thin, let it dry, then roll up like jelly cakes, cut in strips and cook ten or fifteen minutes.

Mrs. A. R. Abbott.

Pea Soup.

Three quarts of water to a pint of split peas, boil until they are soft, strain and return to kettle with a small piece of salt pork. Season with salt pepper and a little sugar.

Miss C. Long.

Tomato Soup.

Three quarts of pork stock, and one quart of tomatoes, sifted half cup of rice. Season with salt, pepper and sugar. Just before serving add a cupful of milk.

Miss C. Long.

Tomato Soup.

Stew six good sized tomatoes as for the table, add pepper, salt and butter. Scald one quart of milk, and when it comes to a boil add the tomato, having added a pinch of soda. Break up crackers and put in.

Mrs. H. Hovey.

Dumplings for Soup.

One pint flour, two small teaspoons baking powder, one half teaspoon salt, one teaspoon sugar, one small cup milk. Mix and roll about half an inch thick. Put them in when the soup is boiling, and cook ten minutes, being careful that the soup does not stop boiling.

Mrs. M. J. Shattuck.

PUDDING.

Strawberry Pudding.

Take one half box of good gelatine and soak in one half pint of water one hour, then add one cup sugar and one pint of boiling water and stir all together. When it is nearly cold, stir in one quart of fresh strawberries. Turn into a mould or deep dish and set away to harden overnight. In the morning make a boiled custard of one quart of milk and reserving the whites of three for frosting, a pinch of salt and a cup of sugar. Put this in a cool place. Just before serving beat the whites to a froth and drop into hot milk to set. Turn the custard over the gelatine, dot the custard and serve. Any other kind of fruit may be used.

MISS. C. LONG.

Corn Starch Pudding.

To one pint of boiling water add three tablespoonfuls corn starch, two tablespoonfuls sugar and a little salt. Beat the whites of three eggs to a stiff froth and stir into it; while boiling add juice of one lemon

MRS. H. HOVEY.

Bird's Nest Pudding.

One half cup butter, one cup sugar, two cups flour, one half cup milk two eggs, two teaspoons baking powder. Put a layer of the cake in a tin, then a layer of sliced apple, then the rest of the cake. Bake an hour in a slow oven. Serve with the following sauce. One cup water, one half cup sugar, one teaspoon flour. When a little cool add one beaten egg, a little butter and flavor with lemon or vanilla.

MRS. WELLS.

After Thought Pudding.

One pint of nice apple sauce sweetened to taste, the yolks of two eggs beaten with it. Put into a buttered dish and bake ten or fifteen minutes. Beat the whites of the eggs to a stiff froth and add half a cup of fine sugar. Spread over the top and return to oven to brown.

MRS. A. G. KIRBY.

Batter Pudding.

Three eggs, one pint milk, nine tablespoonfuls flour, salt and bake half an hour.

MRS. H. HOVEY.

Everybody use Royal Baking Powder.

The Undersigned takes pleasure in informing you that he has established a

CREAMERY

In Dracut, and is now prepared to furnish

PURE MILK, SWEET SKIM MILK, BUTTER MILK,

Milk Delivered Daily at the House of the Customers.

A large experience in the Dairy business enables me to assure entire satisfaction to all my patrons. Your orders solicited.

F. L. PEABODY,

Proprietor Dracut Creamery.

P. O. Box 180, Lowell.

Portland Pudding.

One cup molasses, one cup chopped raisins, one cup sweet milk, one half cup sugar, one teaspoon of clove, one teaspoonful of cinnamon one half a nutmeg, two teaspoons cream of tartar, one teaspoon soda, one teaspoon salt, two eggs, three cups flour. Steam two hours and a half.

MRS. PALMER.

Tapioca Pudding.

Three tablespoons of tapioca, one quart of milk, one tablespoon of butter, two eggs, a little salt. Cook the tapioca in a little water until soft. When cool add the other ingredients and bake half an hour.

C.

Circassian Pudding.

Boil six tablespoons of dried bread crumbs in one pint of milk, stir in the yolks of three eggs beaten with six tablespoons of sugar and a piece of butter as large as an English walnut. Take from the fire, and stir in the beaten whites of three eggs. Flavor with vanilla. When the mixture is cool, pour in a buttered dish and baka slowly until it is set.

MRS. A. G. KIRBY.

Cracker Pudding.

Two scant cups of powdered cracker, one quart of milk, three eggs, spices, salt and sugar. Beat the yolks of the eggs and mix with the pudding, and add the grated rind of a lemon. When the pudding is baked, let it cool a few minutes, then beat the whites of the eggs to a stiff froth with one and a half cups of sugar and the juice of one lemon. Pour over the top and brown in a quick oven.

MRS. H. HOVEY.

Light Plum Pudding.

Cut baker's brick loaf in slices, cutting off all crusts. Butter and lay in layers in a deep earthen dish, with raisins, currants, and citron between. Make a custard of four or five eggs to a quart of milk and one and a half cups sugar; salt and nutmeg to taste. Pour over the bread, and bake two hours or more.

Sauce. Rub well together a cup of sugar and a tablespoon of butter. Add a few drops of hot water at a time, and beat until it creams. Flour to taste.

MRS. L. G. BARRETT.

Cottage Pudding.

On cup sugar, two eggs, one quarter cup butter, one cup milk, one pint flour, two teaspoonfuls cream of tartar, one teaspoon soda, one teaspoon lemon.

MRS. PALMER.

Charlotte Russe Pudding.

Heat one and a half pints of milk to near the boiling point, stir into milk the yolks of four eggs, one half cup sugar and one half tablespoonful corn starch dissolved in a little cold milk, let thicken like custard, and flavor with vanilla. Lay slices of sponge cake in a deep dish and pour the custard over it. When cool beat the four whites and sweeten with one half cup of sugar, spread over pudding and brown in oven. This is very nice.

F. M. C.

Mrs. W's Bread Pudding.

Soak a cup of bread crumbs in a quart of milk two hours, then stir in a small half cup of molasses, a teaspoonful of cinnamon, a little salt, one egg, piece of butter the size of a walnut, half cup raisins. Bake in the oven.

K.

Snow Pudding.

Pour one pint of boiling water on one half a box of Cox's gelatine; after the gelatine is dissolved, add the juice of two lemons, and two cups sugar; strain through a bag when nearly cold. Beat all with the whites ot three eggs nearly an hour, make a soft custard with the yolks of two eggs, one pint of milk, flavor with vanilla. Pour the custard over the pudding just before servfng.

K.

Peach Pudding.

Pare and slice thin five peaches, place in a deep dish and pour over them the following mixture. One cup sugar; one pint milk, boiled together, then add the yolks of two eggs, two tablespoons corn starch, two tablespoons sugar. When cool beat whites of eggs for frosting.

K.

ADAMS & FARLEY,

Book and Job Printers

AND PUBLISHERS.

CALL AND SEE US WHEN IN NEED OF

Cards, Plain or Fancy Tickets, Receipts, Wedding Cards and Invitations, Circulars, Pamphlets, Rent Bills, Letter Heads, Note Heads, Etc., Etc.

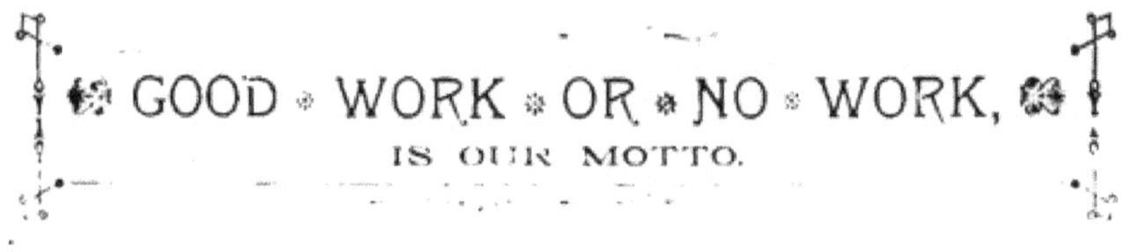

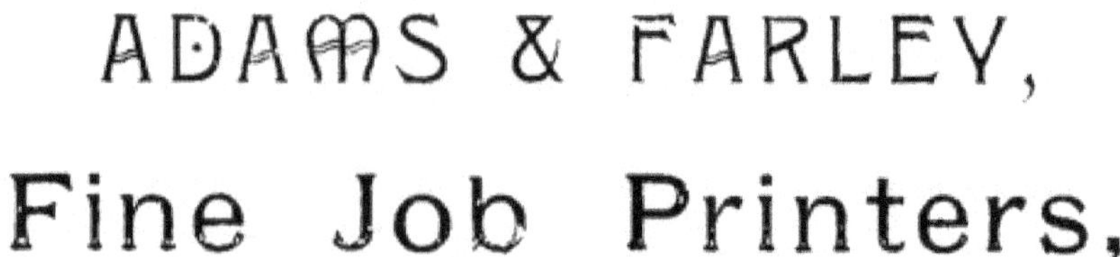

No. 83 Middle Street,

LOWELL, - - - MASS.

Indian Pudding.

Five tablespoons Indian meal, one coffee cup molasses, two eggs, one teaspoon salt beaten together. Boil one quart of milk, pour on above ingredients and bake slowly two or three hours.

K.

Charlotte Russe.

One pint of cream beaten stiff, whites of two eggs well beaten, stir in half a cup powdered sugar and flavor with lemon or vanilla. Let it cool before pouring on cake.

K.

Queen of Puddings.

One pint of nice bread crumbs, one quart of milk, one cup of sugar, the yolks of four eggs, the grated rind of one lemon, a piece of butter the size of an egg. Bake like a custard. Spread slices of jelly of any kind over the top and cover the whole with the whites of eggs beaten to a stiff froth with one cup of sugar, and the juice of the lemon. Brown slightly in the oven.

Z.

Lemon Pudding.

Pour one quart boiling milk over one pint of fine bread crumbs. Let stand a half hour, then add yolks of three eggs, two large tablespoons sugar, and the grated rind of half a lemon. Stir, bake slowly about an hour. Let the pudding cool a few minutes, then spread a layer of jelly over it, and cover with frosting made of the whites of three eggs, one half cup of sugar, and the juice of one lemon beaten together. Brown slightly in the oven.

A Friend.

Creamy Sauce.

One half cup butter, one cup powdered sugar, four tablespoons cream or milk, one teaspoon vanilla, three additional teaspoons milk or cream. Beat the butter to a cream, add sugar gradually and milk gradually. Place the bowl in which the sauce has been made in a dish of boiling water, stir a few minutes until it is smooth and is ready to serve.

Mrs. Hovey.

Foaming Sauce.

Beat half a cup of butter to a cream, add one cup granulated sugar, stir until white and foaming. Just before serving pour a cup of boiling water on it and stir a moment.

MRS. A. G. KIRBY.

Strawberry Dessert.

Fills cups loosely with strawberries, and pour over them corn starch blanc-mange to fill the interstices between the berries. When cold turn out and serve with sugar and cream.

DELLA A. BEAN.

Apple Pudding.

Pare six large apples, take out cores, place in a deep dish and pour custard or light batter over them. Bake one hour. To be eaten with sauce.

DELLA. A. BEAN.

Pudding Sauce.

One cup sugar, two cups hot water, one egg, a little salt, one heaping tablespoon flour. Stir the flour and sugar together dry, then stir into the water slowly and set on stove to boil. After cooking thoroughly stir in the beaten egg, and remove from stove immediately. Flavor to taste.

MRS. M. I. SHATTUCK.

Blueberry Pudding.

Sweeten a quart of canned blueberries to taste, and set on stove in a porcelain kettle. Make a crust of a pint of flour, two small teaspoons baking powder, one teaspoon sugar, one half teaspoon salt, and a small cup of milk. Cut into small cakes, drop into the boiling berries, and steam till done.

MRS. LUCY E. SHAW.

Chocolate Pudding.

Put one and a half pints of milk, one cup sugar into a tin pail placed in a kettle of boiling water. Put one half pint of milk into a sauce-pan, add a heaping tablespoon grated chocolate, boil slowly a few minutes. Wet a tablespoon corn starch in two tablespoons milk, stir into the boiling milk in the pail, add chocolate after straining, and the beaten yolks of three eggs, stir until smooth, flavor, frost with the whites of three eggs, and a teaspoonful of sugar.

MRS. HYDE.

CAKES.

Layer Cakes.

Three eggs, three tablespoons butter, one cup sugar, one cup flour, three tablespoons milk, one teaspoon cream of tartar, and one half teaspoon soda.

MRS. C. W. NEVERS.

Chocolate Cake.

One half cup butter, one cup sugar, one and one half cups flour, one half cup milk, two eggs, one teaspoon cream of tartar, one half teaspoon soda, and two and one half tablespoons chocolate.

MRS. C. W. NEVERS.

Mountain Cake.

One cup sugar, two eggs, one half cup butter, one half cup milk or water, two cups flour, one teaspoon cream of tartar, and one half teaspoon soda. Flavor with nutmeg.

MRS. CAVERLY.

Jelly - Roll.

Three eggs, one cup sugar, two cups flour, one half cup cold water, two teaspoons Royal Baking Powder mixed into the flour. Beat eggs with a beater two minutes, add the sugar, and beat with a spoon five minutes, add half the flour and stir thoroughly, then the water and mix well, then stir in the remainder of the flour. Bake in a shallow pan ten by sixteen inches. When done turn out on a damp cloth, spread with jelly and roll immediately.

MRS. F. W. COBB.

Marble Cake.

White part.—One half cup butter, one half cup milk, one cup white sugar, two cups flour, whites of three eggs, one teaspoon cream of tartar, and one half teaspoon soda.

Dark part.—Yolks of three eggs, one half cup butter, one cup molasses, two and one half cups flour, one half cup milk, one teaspoon cream of tartar, one half teaspoon soda, one quarter spoon each of clove, cinnamon and nutmeg.

MRS. CAVERLY.

Picnic Cake.

Two eggs, and white of one more, three cups sugar, one cup butter, three cups flour, one cup milk, one tablespoon cream of tartar, and one half teaspoon of soda.

MRS. C. W. NEVERS.

Spring Roll.

Four eggs, one cup sugar, one cup flour, one half teaspoon soda, and one of cream of tartar. Flavor to taste. Bake quickly, turn out, spread with jelly, and roll immediately.

MISS. C. LONG.

Nice Marble Cake.

White part.—Two cups white sugar, three cups flour, one half cup butter, one cup sweet milk, whites of five eggs, two teaspoons Royal Baking Powder.

Dark part.—One tablespoon butter, two thirds of a cup of brown sugar, one half cup molasses, one cup raisins, yolks of three eggs, one half teaspoonful soda, one half teaspoon of each kind of spice, and flour to make very stiff.

MRS. F. M. LEWIS.

Angel Cake.

Beat the whites of six eggs to a stiff froth, two thirds cup sugar, one half cup flour after sifting four times, one half teaspoon cream of tartar, in flour, one half teaspoon vanilla.

MRS. S. M. MILLIKEN.

Union Cake.

One cup butter, two cups sugar, one cup milk, three cups flour, one half cup corn starch, four eggs, two teaspoons cream of tartar, one teaspoon soda, two teaspoons extract of lemon.

F. M. C.

Chocolate Sponge Cake.

One cup sugar, two eggs, one square of chocolate, one half cup sweet milk, one teaspoon Royal Baking Powder. Put the chocolate where it will melt, then add the milk. Beat the yolks of the eggs, and stir in sugar and flour with baking powder, then add the beaten whites and lastly the milk, and chocolate.

MRS. S. M. MILLIKEN.

Nice Cheap Fruit Cake.

One cup butter, two cups sugar, two cups sour milk, two cups raisins, five cups flour, one teaspoon soda, salt, cassia, cloves. Citron to taste. This makes two loaves.

F. M. C.

Tea Cake.

Two cups of sugar, one cup of butter, one cup of milk, three eggs, three cups of flour, one teaspoonful cream of tartar, and one half teaspoon of soda. Beat the butter and sugar together, add beaten yolks, then the beaten whites, add the soda dissolved in milk, and stir in flour and cream of tartar last.

Mrs. S. M. Milliken.

Filling For Cake, No. 1.

One cup of figs cut fine, one half cup water, cook until thick, then add two-thirds of a cup of sugar, and boil a few minutes. Cool before using.

Mrs. S. M. Milliken.

No. 2.

One cup powdered sugar, one quarter of a cup of water, simmer gently until it is stiff when dropped into water, the white of one egg, one half cup each of chopped raisins, and walnut meats, a tablespoon of cocoanut, and a few drops of vanilla.

Mrs. S. M. Milliken.

Snow Cake.

Whites of five eggs beaten to a stiff froth, two thirds tumbler of white sugar, one half tumbler flour, and one half teaspoon cream of tartar.

K.

Ribbon Cake.

Two and a half cups sugar, two and a half cups flour, two teaspoons cream of tartar, one teaspoon soda, one cup butter, one cup milk, four eggs. Make three parts. To one part add one cup raisins, one cup currants, and spice to taste.

Mrs. Coburn.

White Cake.

Three cups sugar, one cup butter, one cup milk, one cup flour, one teaspoon cream of tartar, one half teaspoon soda, one cup cornstarch.

K.

Fruit Cake.

Five and a half cups flour, four eggs, two cups sugar, one and a half cups molasses, one and a half cups butter, one cup sweet milk, one teaspoon saleratus, one lb. raisins, one lb. currants, ½lb. citron.

K.

Tumbler Cake.

One tumbler each of sugar, molasses, milk and butter, four eggs, five tumblers flour, one teaspoon soda, one pounds raisins, one pound currants, citron and spice to taste.

MRS. PALMER.

Frosting for Cake.

One tablespoon gelatine soaked in one tablespoon cold water half an hour, add one tablespoon boiling water, and one cup of powdered sugar. Flavor to taste and spread on cake while warm.

K.

To prevent cake from falling, let the tin drop suddenly on the table two or three times before baking.

K.

Raisin Cake.

One cup sugar, one half cup butter, one cup milk, three cups flour, two eggs, one cup chopped raisins, two teaspoons Royal Baking Powder.

MRS. F. W. COBB.

Sponge Cake.

Three eggs beaten five minutes, add one and a half cups sugar, beat ten minutes, one half cup cold water, with one half teaspoon soda dissolved in it, two cups flour sifted four or five times, one teaspoon cream of tartar mixed with it, and one teaspoon of lemon.

A FRIEND.

Jelly Cake.

Stir well together three well beaten eggs, one cup powdered sugar, one cup flour, one teaspoon cream of tartar, mixed with the flour, one half teaspoon of soda dissolved in three tablespoons of water. Spread in two pans and bake. When done turn bottom side up on a napkin, spread with jelly, roll quickly, and wrap in napkin.

A Friend.

Tea Cake.

One egg, one cup sugar, one cup sweet milk, one and a half cups flour, one teaspoon cream of tartar, one half teaspoon soda, and a piece of butter the size of an egg.

Mrs. I. Barnard Brown.

Sponge Cake.

Four eggs beaten a little, one and one half cups sugar, two teaspoons cream of tartar, and one teaspooon soda dissolved in a half cup cold water, stir to a foam, and mix with eggs and sugar. Add two and a half cups flour, and beat well. Bake in a quick oven.

Mrs. I. Barnard Brown.

Fig Cake.

One cup sugar, one half cup butter, two eggs, one half cup milk, one half teaspoon soda, one teaspoon cream of tartar, two cups flour. Bake in three sheets. Take half a pound of figs chopped fine, add the whites of two eggs beaten stiff, and three-fourths of a cup of sugar. Put on the stove in a kettle of hot water, stir till well mixed, then spread between the layers, and on the top. This is very nice.

Mrs. D. N. Patterson.

Cheap Fruit Cake.

Five and a half cups flour, four eggs, two cups sugar, one cup molasses, one and one half cups butter, one cup milk, one teaspoon soda, one pound raisins, two teaspoons cinnamon, one small teaspoon each of clove and mace.

Mrs. M. I. Shattuck.

French Cake.

Three eggs, two cups sugar, one cup sweet milk, one half cup butter, three cups flour, three teaspoons Royal Baking Powder, two teaspoons lemon extract.

MRS. MARY PATTERSON.

Frosting without Eggs.

One cup sugar, four tablespoons milk, set on the stove, and stir constantly until it boils. Boil without stirring five minutes. Take from stove and stir until cold. Chocolate frosting may be made like the above with a small teaspoon of Baker's Breakfast cocoa added while boiling.

MRS. M. I. SHATTUCK.

Snowball Cake.

One cup sugar, one half cup butter, two cups flour, one half cup milk, whites of three eggs, two teaspoons Royal Baking Powder.

MRS. B. B HART

Walnut Cake.

One cup sugar, one half cup butter, one cup milk, three cups flour, two eggs, two teaspoons Royal Baking Powder, one cup chopped walnuts.

MRS. B. B. HART.

Cake to Keep.

Two cups sugar, one cup butter, three cups flour, one third cup milk, five eggs, one teaspoon Royal Baking Powder. Beat butter and sugar together, add yolks of eggs, flour, baking powder and milk. Beat whites of eggs to a stiff froth and stir in last.

MRS. BELLE A. FARDICK.

Dried Apple Cake.

Two cups of dried apples soaked over night. Chop, and stew in two cups of molasses three hours, add two eggs, one cup each of milk, sugar, and butter, one teaspoon soda, a little salt, spices of all kinds, and flour to make the consistency of soft gingerbread.

MRS. B. B. HART.

Circle Cake.

One egg, one cup sugar, two cups flour, one third cup butter, one half cup sweet milk, one teaspoon cream of tartar, one half teaspoon soda. Flavor with rose or lemon. If steamed this may be used for a pudding.

MRS. A. R. ABBOTT.

Aunt Betsey's Cake.

One cup butter, two cups sugar, one cup molasses, five cups flour, one and one half cups cold water two eggs, one nutmeg, one pint chopped raisins, one teaspoon each of soda, salt and clove. Bake one and a half hours in a slow oven. Two loaves.

N. B. Begin the baking between four and five, p. m.

DEA. G. LEIGHTON.

Year Cake.

One cup sugar, one cup butter, one cup molasses, three cups of flour, four eggs, one half pound currants, one half pound raisins, one quarter pound citron, one quarter teaspoon saleratus, one teaspoon each of all kinds of spices.

MRS. H. HOVEY.

Currant Cake.

Two cups flour, one cup sugar, one half cup butter, one half cup milk, two eggs, one teaspoon cream of tartar, one half teaspoon soda. Currants.

MRS. H. HOVEY.

Ribbon Cake.

Two cups sugar, three eggs, two thirds cup butter, one cup sweet milk, three cups flour, one teaspoon saleratus dissolved in the milk, and a little salt. Flavor with lemon or almond. Put half the above in two tins, and to the remainder add two tablespoons of molasses, one teaspoon cinnamon, one half teaspoon clove, a little nutmeg, and a tablespoon of flour.

MISS HELEN RICHARDSON.

MRS. L. A. GROVER,

LADIES' AND GENTS'

Oyster and Dining Rooms,

16 and 18 Merrimack St., Lowell.

Meals Served at all Hours.

OPEN SUNDAYS.

MANDRAKE

Is composed of the concentrated extracts of Mandrake, Yellow Dock, Dandelion, Sarsaparilla, Burdock, Buchu, Hops, Gentian, Chamomile, Red Clover, Stillingia, etc., and will be beneficial in all complaints, arising from a disordered Stomach, Torpidity of the Liver, a Constipated state of the Bowels, and a Scrofulous or other impurities of the blood.

Prepared by

G. C. BROCK, - DRUGGIST,

Lowell, Mass.

Cream Cakes.

To one cup of boiling water, add one half cup of butter. While boiling on the stove, add one cup of flour, and stir until very stiff and smooth, then put away to cool. When cold add four eggs whole and stir until thoroughly mixed. Drop into one dozen cakes on a buttered tin leaving an inch of space around each one. Reserve a little white of egg to brush over top just before putting in oven. Bake about half an hour in a moderate oven.

Cream.—One pint of milk, one egg, six heaping teaspoons flour, one half cup of sugar, and a pinch of salt. Flavor with lemon.

MRS. WELLS.

Chocolate Cake.

One and a half cups of sugar, piece of butter the size of an English walnut, two eggs, one cup of milk or water, in which a scant teaspoon of soda is dissolved, two scant teaspoons cream of tartar, and flour to make a thin batter. Flavor and bake in three small tins. For the filling cut one square of Baker's chocolate in small pieces, put in a sauce pan with a little hot water, let it melt, add a little butter, flavor with a few drops of vanilla, and when cool spread between the cake.

A FRIEND.

Caramel Cake.

Two eggs, one cup sugar, one half cup milk, one half cup butter, two cups flour, one teaspoon cream of tartar, one half teaspoon saleratus. Vanilla. Bake in three sheets.

Caramel.—Two cups sugar, two thirds cup milk, butter the size of an egg. Boil until it begins to harden, then stir until almost cold. Flavor with vanilla and spread over cake.

MRS. N. C. MALLORY, Aurora, Ill.

Fruit Cake.

One cup butter, one cup brown sugar, one cup molasses, one cup milk, three cups flour, four eggs, one half teaspoon cream of tartar, one teaspoon soda, one pound raisins, well chopped, and one nutmeg. This makes two loaves, and will keep six months.

MISS. C. LONG.

A Nice Cake.

Three and a half cups sugar, five cups flour, one cup butter, one cup milk, six eggs, two teaspoons cream of tartar, and one of soda.

MRS. A. G. KIRBY.

Date Cake.

Four eggs, one small cup butter, two cups sugar, one cup milk, two teaspoons cream of tartar, one teaspoon soda, three cups flour, and one pound of dates cut up. We recommend this very highly.

MISS C. LONG.

Chocolate Cake.

Two eggs, one half cup of sugar, butter size of an egg, one half cup milk, one cup flour, one teaspoon cream of tartar, one half teaspoon of soda. Beat the whites and yolks of eggs separately.

Frosting. One egg and one tablespoon flour beaten together, one large cup of milk, three quarters cup of sugar, one half cup of grated chocolate. Dissolve the chocolate in water, turn the milk in and boil ten minutes, then turn in the rest, and boil five minutes. Flavor with vanilla.

X.

Cup Cake.

Three cups of sugar, one cup of butter, one cup sweet milk, four eggs, five cups of flour, one teaspoon cream of tartar, one half teaspoon soda, a tumbler of citron. Flavor with lemon.

MISS C. LONG.

Sponge Cake.

Beat the whites and yolks of four eggs separately. To the yolks add one cup of sugar, and a small teaspoon of Royal Baking Powder, and beat five minutes, then cut rather than beat in the whites of eggs, stopping the minute they are evenly mixed. Then add one cup of flour and stir no more than necessary to mix it in. Flavor if preferred. Bake in a moderate oven about half an hour, or until it will not stick to a broom splint.

MRS. C. W. WELLS.

Dayton Cake.

One and one half cups sugar, one third cup butter, one third cup milk, three cups flour, three eggs, one half teaspoon cream of tartar, one half teaspoon soda and one nutmeg.

MRS. CAVERLY.

Pound Cake.

One and one half cups sugar, one and one half cups flour, one cup butter, five eggs, one half teaspoon of Royal Baking Powder. Melt the butter and stir into the flour, then add the beaten eggs and sugar, and stir till free from lumps, then add baking powder.

MRS. NEVERS.

Sponge Cake.

Three eggs, beat two minutes, one and one half cups sugar, beat five minutes; one cup flour, one teaspoon cream tartar, beat two minutes; one half cup cold water, one half teaspoon soda, beat one minute; add one large cup flour, salt and flavor to taste. Bake twenty minutes. This makes two loaves.

MRS. SYLVESTER BEAN.

MISCELLANEOUS.

Jellies.

For every pint of juice take a pint of sugar. Heat sugar in a pan in an open oven, or where it will get too hot to handle. Boil fruit juice, twenty five minutes, stir in hot sugar, and boil five minutes.

Z.

Baked Hams.

Take a small or medium sized ham, trimmed into good shape. The evening previous to cooking, soak in a pan of hot water three or four hours. In the morning make a stiff paste of rye meal, mixed with water, and cover the ham entirely with the paste. Bake five or six hours in a moderate oven. When done remove crust, take off skin, and dredge with powdered bread crumbs. Save the skin to cover the cold ham when it is put away.

K.

Beef Tea.

Cut half a pound of lean beef, into very small pieces and put it into a wide mouthed bottle, add half a cup of cold water, and cork tightly. Put the bottle in a basin of cold water, and place on the fire where it will come to the boiling point, but not boil. Keep at this temperature two hours, then strain, and season with salt. Q.

Doughnuts.

One cup sugar, one egg, salt, nutmeg, two tablespoons each of melted lard, and cream of tartar, one teaspoon soda, stir in flour, care being taken not to get in too much.

F. M. C.

Merricks.

Two eggs, two tablespoons each of butter, and sugar, flour to mix stiff, roll thin and fry in hot lard as doughnuts.

DELLA A. BEAN.

Appropiate Holiday Dish, Happy Woman "A La Mode."

Take one piece of silk with smaller quantity of brocade satin to correspond, stir in buttons to match, also spool of silk, twist, braid, etc., use a bit of canvass for stiffening; season with laces, ribbons or other trimmings to suit the taste roll in one of Grant & Cobb's wrappers, and put in a dark closet to serve for breakfast Christmas morning; with side dishes of jewelry, furs, gloves, etc. This dish may be made of less expensive ingredients, and still make a Happy Woman.

To Keep Eggs.

To four quarts of air slacked lime, put two tablespoons cream of tartar, two of salt, and four quarts of cold water. Put fresh eggs into a tight firkin, and pour the mixture over them. The water may settle away so as to leave the upper layer uncovered. If so, add more of the mixture, cover closely and keep in a cool place.

I have put down eggs this way for twenty years, in summer, for winter use and have never found a poor one.

Mrs. M. I. Shattuck.

Veal Loaf.

Two pounds lean veal, after it is boiled. Chop fine, add three well beaten eggs, three pounded crackers, one half tablespoon salt, one half of black pepper. Moisten with the water in which the meat was boiled. Bake in a bread pan half an hour. Slice cold.

A Friend.

Spiced Berries.

Eights quarts blueberries, four pounds brown sugar, one q' art vinegar, one tablespoon each of clove, allspice, and cinnamon. Crush the berries, add the sugar, vinegar, and spices. Let boil till it begins to thicken.

A Friend.

A Nice Varnish.

Two ounces gum shellac, put into one half pint alcohol. This makes old furniture look like new.

Miss. C. Long.

Breakfast Dishes.

Place the gem pan on the hottest part of the stove, while stirring together two teacups each, of flour and Indian meal, one pint of milk, one teaspoon soda, two teaspoons cream of tartar, two tablespoons sugar, and a little salt. Beat quickly. Pour batter in pan, and when it begins to rise, put on grate in oven.

Meats left over from dinner may be chopped, seasoned with one part sugar, and two parts mustard wet up with vinegar.

Cold boiled potatoes, sliced, and toasted brown are palatable.

Pan Dowdy.

Slice twelve apples pretty thick, put two slices of pork in a pot and fry out slowly. Make a cream of tartar paste. Put a layer of apples, and then a layer of paste, and so on till all is used. Add half a cup of molasses, half a cup of sugar, and a cup of cold water, cook three-quarters of an hour.

MRS. H. HOVEY.

Apple Pan Cakes.

Two cups of sweet milk, one egg, two tablespoons sugar, half a teaspoon soda, same of salt, flour for a thin batter, two good sized apples, pare, and slice into the batter. Drop into hot fat.

H.

To prevent fruit jars from cracking, place a tablespoon in the jar while filling with hot fruit.

Oyster Chowder.

One pint oysters, one quart milk, two potatoes, one large onion, butter size of an egg, salt, pepper, and one teaspoon flour.

MRS. WELLS.

Welsh Rarebit.

One pound of cheese, two eggs, one half teaspoon mustard, one quarter teaspoon salt, a little pepper, one tablespoon melted butter, one half cup milk. Break the cheese in small pieces, and put it, with all the other ingredients in a bright sauce pan, which put over boiling water. Stir until the cheese meets then spread on slices of crisp toast and serve immediately.

MRS. WELLS.

Rice Mush.

One cup rice, half a cup of corn meal, a little salt, well cooked in a pint and a half of milk or water. When cold cut into slices, and bake or fry. Serve hot.

MRS. M. C. COLE.

Omelet.

Three eggs, whites and yolks beaten separately, half a teacup milk, one tablespoon flour, half of butter, pepper and salt to taste. Stir the flour into half of the milk, and melt the butter in the other half; put the whites in last. Bake in jelly pans, and serve hot.

MRS. M. C. COLE.

Baked Eggs.

Break eggs into a buttered dish, far enough apart for the yolks not to touch each other, sprinkle with salt and pepper, putting a little butter on each if wished. Bake until the whites set. Serve hot on toast.

MRS. M. C. COLE.

Escaloped Tomatoes.

Scald and remove skins of fully ripe tomatoes. Cover the bottom of a buttered pudding dish with a layer of sliced tomatoes seasoned with pepper and salt, cover with pepper and salt, cover with a layer of bread and butter, and so on until the dish is full, finishing with the tomatoes. Bake one half hour in a moderate oven, and serve hot.

MRS. M. C. COLE.

Fritters.

One pint sour cream or milk, one half teaspoon soda, a little salt. Mix soft with flour.

MRS. B. B. HART.

Cream Fish.

Pick any kind of cold, baked or boiled fish into small pieces, and put in a dish. Take one pint of milk and season to taste, with butter, salt, and pepper; let the milk boil, then thicken with one tablespoon of flour. Pour over the cold fish, and sprinkle with cracker crumbs, and bits of butter. Bake about twenty minutes. This is nice for breakfast or tea.

MRS. D. N. PATTERSON.

Scrambled Codfish.

Pick codfish in pieces, and soak overnight. In the morning add one cup sweet milk; when hot, not boiling, three eggs well beaten, and stirred briskly into the fish. Be careful not to boil it. Season with salt, and pepper.

MRS. M. C. COLE.

Codfish Toast.

Freshen nicely picked codfish by putting in water over night. In the morning, add sweet cream or milk, and butter, and pour over nicely toasted bread.

MRS. M. C. COLE.

Oyster Fritters.

Half a pint sweet milk, two eggs well beaten, flour to make a batter, a little salt and soda. Put in the oysters, and fry in hot butter and lard mixed.

MRS. M. C. COLE.

How to Cook Ham.

Put the ham into cold water, boil slowly five or six hours, then take out and trim for the table. Place in a baking pan and set in a hot oven until brown.

MRS. J. B. BROWN.

Doughnuts.

One cup sugar, one cup milk, one egg, one pinch ginger, and salt, two teaspoons cream of tartar, one of soda, and flour to knead.

MRS. PALMER.

Escaloped Potatoes.

Slice thin cold boiled patatoes. Butter au earthen dish, put in a layer of potatoes and season with pepper, salt and butter, and sprinkle on a little flour. Put another layer of potatoes and seasoning, and so on until the dish is filled. Pour on a cup of milk just before putting in oven. Bake three quarters of an hour.

X.

We have constantly on hand and for sale, in large and small quantities, many articles now considered indispensable in well-regulated families, and call your attention to a few, viz:—

AMMONIA, of full strength. GLYCERINE, chemically pure.

BENZINE, doubly deodorized, for cleaning cloths, Gloves, or most delicate fabrics.

ALCOHOL, ninety-five per cent.

GUM ARABIC, white and common.

GUM CAMPHOR, pure refined.

WAX, sperm and paraffine.

BEES' WAX, white and yellow.

SAL SODA. COPPERAS.

CHLORIDE OF LIME. DISINFECTANT.

SULPHUR. BRIMSTONE.

POTASH. LIME, &c., &c.

SOLUBLE BLUE. A prepared Dry Blue, soluble in water. One-quarter pound will produce the Best Liquid Blue, in sufficient quantity to last a family one year. Would have been recommended without doubt by Miss Parloa had she done washing instead of diplomatic puddings.

STOVE LINING An excellent article, as it saves time, trouble, and expense. A little of it in the house enables one to repair a cracked or broken lining without trouble or delay. We have sold TONS of it, and it gives universal satisfaction.

SOAPS, for laundry and house use.

C. B. COBURN & CO.,

35 MARKET STREET.

Fish Chowder.

For six persons, take three slices of fat pork and fry in the kettle until crisp and brown, then take it out on a plate, add a layer of sliced potatoes, and of sliced onions, and five or six pounds of haddock cut in slices, then a layer of crackers. Repeat these layers, till the kettle is full. Pour on boiling water till it covers the ingredients, boil slowly half an hour, pepper and salt to taste. Add half a pint of milk, and butter the size of an egg, just before serving. A most excellent chowder.

MRS. A. R. ABBOTT.

Fried Apples.

Cut good cooking apples in quarters, put in a hot spider in which a lump of butter has been placed. Sprinkle considerable sugar over them, pour on a very little hot water. Cover closely and serve as soon as cooked.

MRS. C. W. NEVERS.

To Remove Iron Rust.

Rub with dry cream of tartar while the cloth is wet, hang where the sun will shine directly upon it. Repeat the process if necessary.

MRS. C. W. NEVERS.

A New Recipe.

Do you wish a new recipe, simple, delightful?
Breakfast, dinner, or supper appropriate for,
Whose components can always be found in the pantry,
Requiring no visit to cellar or store.

A blessing t'will prove when you're late with your breakfast
When children are fractious or fretful, or Will
Brings home a choice friend from the city to dinner,
And the partridge won't brown, and the kidneys won't gri'll.

Take a gill of forbearance, four ounces of patience,
A pinch of submission, a handful of grace;
Mix well with the milk of the best human kindness!
Serve at once with a radiant smile on your face.

Pray try this new recipe, much burdened house-wives,
It's sure to turn out a most perfect success.
Its name? Why Good Temper, a rich boon from Heaven,
Our souls and our spirits to comfort and bless.

Baked Macaroni.

Cut in small pieces, turn on boiling water, add one teaspoon salt, boil twenty minutes, turn into a sieve, and wash thoroughly with cold water. Butter a pudding dish, put in a layer of macaroni, pieces of butter, pepper and salt, grated cheese, and so continued until the macaroni is used. Cover with milk and bake slowly. Very nice.

MRS. C. W. NEVERS.

Pork Hash.

Chop fried salt pork fine, and mix with cold mashed potatoes, two hard boiled eggs, well chopped, two slices bread cut up fine. Stir all together with hot fat; let it remain long enough to brown underneath. Serve with the brown portion on top. It is very appetizing for breakfast.

MRS. C. W. NEVERS.

Crab Apple Jelly.

Wash the apples, cover with water, let boil until tender, drain through cheese cloth. To every four cups juice add five cups sugar. Let the juice boil before adding sugar, then about two minutes after sugar is added. Put at once into glass.

MRS. H. SWANN.

Citron Preserve.

Pare the citron, boil in water in which a little piece of alum has been dissolved, boil until perfectly tender, sprinkle with sugar and let remain over night. In the morning cut in small pieces, remove seeds, and to every pound of fruit add three quarters of a pound of sugar. Boil slowly until the fruit is a rich yellow. Cool in stone jar before covering.

MRS. H. SWANN.

Lobster Salad.

One lobster, one head lettuce, three eggs, two tablespoons butter, one tablespoon mustard, two teaspoons salt, one of red pepper. Chop lobster, and lettuce fine, add salt, pepper and mustard. Boil the eggs hard, chop fine, warm the butter, and add last. Moisten the whole with vinegar.

MRS. H. SWANN.

Roast Turkey.

Having dressed carefully rub inside with salt, hang up to drain one hour, if you have time then wipe dry. Make the dressing of bread crumbs seasoned with salt, pepper, sage, butter, or pork chopped fine, one egg, one half an onion chopped. Wet all with water. Fill the crop first and sew up; then the body. Tie the legs to the body, rub the turkey with butter partly melted as this will give it a nice brown. Bake one and a half to two hours or more, according to size. Baste often.

MRS. BARKER.

Doughnuts.

Three pints of flour, two teaspoons cream of tartar, one of soda, piece of butter the size of an English Walnut, two eggs, one cup sugar, a little nutmeg, and milk enough to moisture. Beat the eggs separately.

MISS. IRA SWEATT.

A Recipe for Salad.

To make this condiment, your poet begs
The pounded yellow of two hard boiled eggs;
Two boiled potatoes, pass'd through kitchen sieve,
Smoothness and softness to the salad give;
Let onion atoms lurk within the bowl,
And half suspected, animate the whole;
Of mordant mustard add a single spoon,
Distrust the condiment that bites so soon;
But, deem it not, thou man of herbs, a fault
To add a double quantity of salt;
Four times the spoon with oil from Lucca crown,
And twice with vinegar produced from town;
And, lastly, o'er the flavored compound toss
A magic soupçon of anchovy sauce.
Oh, green and glorious! O, herbaceous treat!
T'would tempt a dying anchorite to eat;
Back to the world he'd turn his fleeting soul,
And plunge his fingers in the salad bowl!
Serenely full the epicure would say,
"Fate cannot harm me, I have dined to-day."

SYDNEY SMITH.

Ice Cream.

One pint milk, three eggs, one half cup flour, one half cup sugar; scald all together. When cold add one pint of cream and a pinch of salt. Very nice.

MRS. M. J. STUDLEY.

Citron Preserve.

Pare and cut the citron into small blocks, and boil in clear water until perfectly tender. Place the fruit in a culendar and drain. Throw away the water. Make a rich syrup of four lbs. of sugar to five lbs. of the fruit, add a little water, and cook until it is thick, (this takes but a short time.) Add to the syrup the fruit, and lemons boiled tender then sliced. Allow the whole to boil a few minutes, and then can it. Use about three lemons to five lbs of the fruit.

MRS. L. G. BARRETT.

Raspberry Jam.

Mash the berries, place them on the stove, boil them fifteen minutes, add three quarters of a lb. sugar to each pound of fruit, and boil twenty minutes. Put up in tumblers.

MRS. L. G. BARRETT.

Buns.

At noon mix one half cup of yeast, one half cup of milk, and one cup of flour. Put in a warm place. At night add one half cup of milk, three quarters cup of sugar, a piece of butter as large as a butternut, and flour to knead. In the morning, add a few currants or chopped raisins, and make into tiny biscuits. Put away to rise. When they are very light, beat a portion of the white of egg, and rub over the top before baking, or put a little melted sugar over them on taking from the oven.

MRS. MARY B. HUBBARD.

Johnny Cake.

One cup Indian meal, one cup sour milk, one half cup flour, one teaspoon soda, and one of salt. Bake quickly.

MRS. THISSELL.

Full of pluck.—Countryman, to dentist: "I shan't pay notin' extra for gas. Jest pull her out if it does hurt." Dentist: "You are plucky sir. Let me see the tooth." Countryman: "O, 'taint me that's got the toothache—it's my wife! She'll be here in a minute."

Painless Dentistry.

Professor, sternly: "I cannot understand, Mr. Jones, how you can be so stupid." Jones: "Perhaps, sir, it is because you have given me a piece of your mind."

Noodle Soup.

Boil a soup bone four or five hours; an hour before dinner beat two eggs well, add flour to make stiff enough for rolling out, roll very thin and let lie half an hour, then cut in thin strips and add to the soup; boil fifteen minutes, and you will have very good noodle soup.

A FRIEND.

"Doctor, when do you think a man weighs most?" asked a patient who was undergoing a course of dietary treatment. "When he steps on my corns," answered the doctor.

Cocoanut Cakes.

One pound of pulverized cocoanut, two cups flour, cup and a half of pulverized sugar. Soak cocoanut over night. Drain all off dry in morning. Beat sugar and the whites of six eggs until almost still enough for frosting. Take greased tissue paper on plate, and drop not more than a teaspoon on a plate.

B. G.

Sugar Candy.

Six cups of granulated sugar, half a cup of vinegar, half a cup of water. Put all on the stove together, and boil (without stirring) until it hardens when dropped in cold water. Flavor with vanilla, and pour into buttered tins. This may be improved by adding English walnuts.

X. Y. Z.

Cream Walnuts.

White of one egg beaten to a froth, and a teaspoon of cold water; stir in enough powdered sugar to make a thick paste; the sugar should be sifted before using. When stiff enough to mould with the hands, form into little balls the size of a cherry, then press the half of an English walnut into the side, and set aside to harden. Vanilla improves this.

X.

The cashier of a business house in New York finds that the following notice, posted in front of his desk, serves as a useful purpos; "Never address your conversation to a person engaged in adding figures. There is nothing so deaf as an adder."

Pop-Corn Balls.

Put a large cup of molasses in a pan, add a small lump of butter, and boil together. Pour over the popped corn, stir well, and press into balls as hot as can be handled. Rub the hands with butter while making the balls.

Z.

Butter Taffy.

Two cups of brown sugar, half a cup of butter, two tablespoons of vinegar, and two of molasses. Boil until it hardens in water, then pour on buttered pans.

CARLOTTA THOMPSON.

A Chicago store displays this legend: "The Truth Spoken here."

"Why, Miss Howjames," said the Chicago girl, "you dont mean that it is all over between you and Mr. Grinshaw?" "What I have told you," replied the Boston lady haughtily, "is the—the undraped actuality."

Breakfast Cake.

One egg, one cup of sweet milk, two cups flour, one cup Indian meal, two tablespoons sugar, two tablespoons cream of tartar, one teaspoon soda.

MRS. C. N. SPENCER.

Johnny Cake.

One cup Indian meal, one cup sour milk, one half cup flour, one teaspoon saleratus, one teaspoon salt. Bake quickly.

Mrs. Thissell.

"I wouldn't cut that tree down if I were you," said a visitor, to a Richland township farmer who was about to chop down a very large oak. "Remember that after you fell it, you cannot replace it." „Can't I," replied the farmer. "You don't know. After I chop it down, what is to prevent me from chopping it up?"—Pittsburg Chronicle.

Cabbage Salad.

Put the milk and the vinegar on to heat in separate sauce-pans; when the vinegar boils, add butter, sugar, salt, and pepper, and stir in the chopped cabbage; cover and let scald and steam—not boil—for a moment, meanwhile remove hot milk from stove, cool a little and stir in the well-beaten and strained yolks. Return to stove and boil a moment. Dish cabbage and pour custard over it, stir rapidly with a silver spoon until well mixed, and set immediately in a cold place.

Buckeye Cook-Book.

Recommended by Mrs. C. N. Nevers.

At an evening party in Cork, a lady said to her partner, "Can you tell me who that exceedingly plain man is sitting opposite to us?" "That is my brother." "Oh, I beg your pardon," she replied, much confused; "I had not noticed the resemblance."

Clam Chowder.

Fry slowly two slices of pork cut into small bits. Add four large potatoes well sliced, two large sliced onions, the clam juice, pepper and salt, if needed, and water enough to cover the mixture. Boil until the potatoes and onions are nearly done, then add a quart of clams taken out of the shells while raw. Boil this mixture a few minutes then add a cup of milk and a little thick ning. Pour over halves of cracker and lumps of butter, and serve at once.

Mrs. F. S. Crawford.

In the village of L. a minister one Sunday when about to publish the bans of marriage, discovered he could not find the names. Not wishing to make a long pause, he repeated, "I publish the bans of marriage between"— Still no signs of the paper. He began again, "I publish the bans of marriage between"—Still no paper could be found. He began once more, "I publish the bans of marriage between"—The beadle, wishing to enlighten him as to where the paper containing the names was, cried out to the consternation of the congregation: "Atween the cushion and the desk, sir."

"What I'd like to know," said a school-boy, "is how the mouths of rivers can be so much larger than their heads."

Pigs in Blankets.

Slice English Bacon very thin, place an oyster in the centre of each slice, pepper and fold together, fastening with two tooth picks crossed. Fry brown without using salt or butter.

MRS. C. N. NEVERS.

Citizen (to coal dealer)—Say, I want a ton of coal. Coal Dealer—All right. Shall we send it up right away? Citizen—Oh, no. If it's anything like the last, I'll just call for it on my way home, and carry it up in my overcoat pocket.—Washington Critic.

To Cook Asparagus.

Cut one bunch of asparagus into inch pieces. Boil until tender in just water enough to cover it. Salt to taste. Pour on a cup of milk, thicken with a spoonful of flour, add a tablespoon butter and three hard boiled eggs sliced thin. Stir gently while it boils a few minutes, then pour over slices of buttered toast.

MRS. F. R. STROUT.

Wife (on her husband's return from his office)—I came across a lot of your old love-letters to-day, dear, in one of the trunks upstairs. Ah, John, how you did love me! Husband—Yes, indeed. Is dinner ready? I'm as hungry as a tramp.—Harper's Bazaar.

Wife—I declare I am almost ashamed to go to church with this hat on. It isn't at all the style. Husband—Is this Bridget's Sunday out? Wife—No. Husband—Why dont you borrow hers?

Cocoanut Cracker Pudding.

Roll three common crackers fine and add one quart milk heated to a scald. Let them soak, while beating yolks of three eggs, three-quarter cup sugar and a pinch of salt. Mix with cracker and milk, then add one cup cocoanut and small piece of butter. Bake in a moderate oven. When done frost with the three whites and brown.

MRS. F. R. STROUT.

According to an old superstition of the mediaeval church, whenever a cock crows, a lie is being told. The reason that cocks crow so persistently in the early morning hours, is because the morning papers are being set up.—Exchange.

Salad Dressing.

One tablespoon mustard, one teaspoon salt, one teaspoon sugar, add four tablespoons boiling water and mix till smooth; add one half cup melted butter, stir thoroughly. Add three beaten eggs, stir rapidly; then half a cup vinegar, stir constantly; add two-thirds cup boiling milk gradually to prevent curdling. Cook in double boiler (must not be tin), till of the consistency of soft custard. This will keep several weeks.

Shreded, or finely chopped raw white cabbage is a very palatable relish served with above dressing. *

A Stuffed Beefsteak.

Prepare bread scalded soft and mixed with plenty of butter and a little pepper and salt. Lay it upon one side of a round of steak, cover with the other, and baste it down with needle and thread. Salt and pepper the outside of the steak and place it in a dripping-pan with half an inch of water. When baked brown on one side, turn, and bake the other.

Fresh milk boiled with loaf-sugar will soothe a cough when other things fail.

HINTS.

The secret of a good day is a good morning, and a good morning always begins the night before. So, many things toward a good start the coming day can be done the hour before you retire.

It is a good plan to wrap cans of fruit in newspapers and put them away in a dark, cool place. The wrapping in paper and keeping dark is said to prevent the bleaching of the fruit.

For stains on the hands nothing is better than a little salt, with enough lemon juice to moisten it, rubbed on the spots and then washed off in clear water.

In a basin of water, salt, of course, falls to the bottom; so never soak salt fish with the skin side down, as the salt will fall to the skin and remain there.

Never Done.

"Men work from morn till set of sun." They do.
"But woman's work is never done." Quite true.
For when one task she's finished, something's found
Awaiting a beginning, all year round.
Whether it be
To draw the tea,
Or bake the bread,
Or make the bed,
Or ply the broom,
Or dust the room,
Or floor to scrub,
Or knives to rub,
Or table to set,
Or meals to get,
Or shelves to scan,
Or fruit to can,
Or seeds to sow,
Or plants to grow,
Or linens to bleach,
Or lessons to teach,
Or butter to churn,
Or jackets to turn,
Or polish glass,
Or plate of brass,
Or clothes to mend,
Or children to tend,
Or notes indite,
Or stories write—
Those oars propel your barks o'er household seas
In sunny heavens where you rest at ease,
And, one word more, don't you forget it, please.

—[Western Plowman.

THE END.

www.ingramcontent.com/pod-product-compliance
Lightning Source LLC
Chambersburg PA
CBHW031450270326
41930CB00007B/933

* 9 7 8 3 7 4 4 7 9 2 5 0 9 *